THIS JOURNAL BELONGS TO:

_____

DATE:

Today I am grateful for:

1.
2.
3.

As I reflect on yesterday, what went well and what goals did I accomplish?

Today's self-care goals:

1.
2.
3.

Affirmations I am declaring today!

SHARE YOUR JOY

Today I am grateful for:

1.
2.
3.

As I reflect on yesterday, what went well and what goals did I accomplish?

Today's self-care goals:

1.
2.
3.

Affirmations I am declaring today!

SHARE YOUR JOY

DATE:

Today I am grateful for:

1. _____
2. _____
3. _____

As I reflect on yesterday, what went well and what goals did I accomplish?

_____
_____
_____
_____

Today's self-care goals:

1. _____
2. _____
3. _____

Affirmations I am declaring today!

_____
_____
_____
_____

SHARE YOUR JOY

Today I am grateful for:

1. ....
2. ....
3. ....

As I reflect on yesterday, what went well and what goals did I accomplish?

_____

_____

_____

Today's self-care goals:

1. ....
2. ....
3. ....

Affirmations I am declaring today!

_____

_____

_____

_____

SHARE YOUR JOY

DATE:

Today I am grateful for:

1.
2.
3.

As I reflect on yesterday, what went well and what goals did I accomplish?

Today's self-care goals:

1.
2.
3.

Affirmations I am declaring today!

SHARE YOUR JOY

Today I am grateful for:

1. ....
2. ....
3. ....

As I reflect on yesterday, what went well and what goals did I accomplish?

_____

_____

_____

Today's self-care goals:

1. ....
2. ....
3. ....

Affirmations I am declaring today!

_____

_____

_____

_____

SHARE YOUR JOY

DATE:

Today I am grateful for:

1. ....
2. ....
3. ....

As I reflect on yesterday, what went well and what goals did I accomplish?

_____

_____

_____

Today's self-care goals:

1. ....
2. ....
3. ....

Affirmations I am declaring today!

_____

_____

_____

_____

SHARE YOUR JOY

Today I am grateful for:

1. ....

2. ....

3. ....

As I reflect on yesterday, what went well and what goals did I accomplish?

_____

_____

_____

Today's self-care goals:

1. ....

2. ....

3. ....

Affirmations I am declaring today!

_____

_____

_____

_____

_____

SHARE YOUR JOY

DATE:

Today I am grateful for:

1. _____
2. _____
3. _____

As I reflect on yesterday, what went well and what goals did I accomplish?

_____

_____

_____

Today's self-care goals:

1. _____
2. _____
3. _____

Affirmations I am declaring today!

_____

_____

_____

_____

SHARE YOUR JOY

DATE:

Today I am grateful for:

1. ....
2. ....
3. ....

As I reflect on yesterday, what went well and what goals did I accomplish?

_____

_____

_____

Today's self-care goals:

1. ....
2. ....
3. ....

Affirmations I am declaring today!

_____

_____

_____

_____

_____

SHARE YOUR JOY

DATE:

Today I am grateful for:

1. ....
2. ....
3. ....

As I reflect on yesterday, what went well and what goals did I accomplish?

_____

_____

_____

Today's self-care goals:

1. ....
2. ....
3. ....

Affirmations I am declaring today!

_____

_____

_____

_____

SHARE YOUR JOY

Today I am grateful for:

1. ....
2. ....
3. ....

As I reflect on yesterday, what went well and what goals did I accomplish?

_____

_____

_____

_____

Today's self-care goals:

1. ....
2. ....
3. ....

Affirmations I am declaring today!

_____

_____

_____

_____

_____

SHARE YOUR JOY

DATE:

Today I am grateful for:

1. ....
2. ....
3. ....

As I reflect on yesterday, what went well and what goals did I accomplish?

_____

_____

_____

Today's self-care goals:

1. ....
2. ....
3. ....

Affirmations I am declaring today!

_____

_____

_____

_____

_____

SHARE YOUR JOY

DATE:

Today I am grateful for:

1. _____
2. _____
3. _____

As I reflect on yesterday, what went well and what goals did I accomplish?

_____

_____

_____

Today's self-care goals:

1. _____
2. _____
3. _____

Affirmations I am declaring today!

_____

_____

_____

_____

_____

SHARE YOUR JOY

DATE:

Today I am grateful for:

1. ....
2. ....
3. ....

As I reflect on yesterday, what went well and what goals did I accomplish?

_____

_____

_____

Today's self-care goals:

1. ....
2. ....
3. ....

Affirmations I am declaring today!

_____

_____

_____

_____

_____

SHARE YOUR JOY

DATE:

Today I am grateful for:

1. ....
2. ....
3. ....

As I reflect on yesterday, what went well and what goals did I accomplish?

_____
_____
_____
_____

Today's self-care goals:

1. ....
2. ....
3. ....

Affirmations I am declaring today!

_____
_____
_____
_____

SHARE YOUR JOY

DATE:

Today I am grateful for:

1. ....
2. ....
3. ....

As I reflect on yesterday, what went well and what goals did I accomplish?

_____

_____

_____

_____

Today's self-care goals:

1. ....
2. ....
3. ....

Affirmations I am declaring today!

_____

_____

_____

_____

SHARE YOUR JOY

Today I am grateful for:

1.
2.
3.

As I reflect on yesterday, what went well and what goals did I accomplish?

Today's self-care goals:

1.
2.
3.

Affirmations I am declaring today!

SHARE YOUR JOY

Today I am grateful for:

1. ....

2. ....

3. ....

As I reflect on yesterday, what went well and what goals did I accomplish?

_____

_____

_____

Today's self-care goals:

1. ....

2. ....

3. ....

Affirmations I am declaring today!

_____

_____

_____

_____

SHARE YOUR JOY

DATE:

Today I am grateful for:

1. ....
2. ....
3. ....

As I reflect on yesterday, what went well and what goals did I accomplish?

_____

_____

_____

_____

Today's self-care goals:

1. ....
2. ....
3. ....

Affirmations I am declaring today!

_____

_____

_____

_____

_____

SHARE YOUR JOY

DATE:

Today I am grateful for:

1. ....
2. ....
3. ....

As I reflect on yesterday, what went well and what goals did I accomplish?

_____

_____

_____

_____

Today's self-care goals:

1. ....
2. ....
3. ....

Affirmations I am declaring today!

_____

_____

_____

_____

_____

SHARE YOUR JOY

DATE:

Today I am grateful for:

1. ....
2. ....
3. ....

As I reflect on yesterday, what went well and what goals did I accomplish?

_____

_____

_____

_____

Today's self-care goals:

1. ....
2. ....
3. ....

Affirmations I am declaring today!

_____

_____

_____

_____

_____

SHARE YOUR JOY

DATE:

Today I am grateful for:

1. ....
2. ....
3. ....

As I reflect on yesterday, what went well and what goals did I accomplish?

_____

_____

_____

Today's self-care goals:

1. ....
2. ....
3. ....

Affirmations I am declaring today!

_____

_____

_____

_____

SHARE YOUR JOY

DATE:

Today I am grateful for:

1. ....
2. ....
3. ....

As I reflect on yesterday, what went well and what goals did I accomplish?

_____

_____

_____

Today's self-care goals:

1. ....
2. ....
3. ....

Affirmations I am declaring today!

_____

_____

_____

_____

SHARE YOUR JOY

DATE:

Today I am grateful for:

1. _____
2. _____
3. _____

As I reflect on yesterday, what went well and what goals did I accomplish?

_____
_____
_____
_____

Today's self-care goals:

1. _____
2. _____
3. _____

Affirmations I am declaring today!

_____
_____
_____
_____

SHARE YOUR JOY

DATE:

Today I am grateful for:

1. ....
2. ....
3. ....

As I reflect on yesterday, what went well and what goals did I accomplish?

_____

_____

_____

Today's self-care goals:

1. ....
2. ....
3. ....

Affirmations I am declaring today!

_____

_____

_____

_____

SHARE YOUR JOY

Today I am grateful for:

1. ....
2. ....
3. ....

As I reflect on yesterday, what went well and what goals did I accomplish?

_____

_____

_____

_____

Today's self-care goals:

1. ....
2. ....
3. ....

Affirmations I am declaring today!

_____

_____

_____

_____

SHARE YOUR JOY

DATE:

Today I am grateful for:

1. ....
2. ....
3. ....

As I reflect on yesterday, what went well and what goals did I accomplish?

_____

_____

_____

Today's self-care goals:

1. ....
2. ....
3. ....

Affirmations I am declaring today!

_____

_____

_____

_____

SHARE YOUR JOY

DATE:

Today I am grateful for:

1. _____
2. _____
3. _____

As I reflect on yesterday, what went well and what goals did I accomplish?

_____
_____
_____
_____

Today's self-care goals:

1. _____
2. _____
3. _____

Affirmations I am declaring today!

_____
_____
_____
_____

SHARE YOUR JOY

DATE:

Today I am grateful for:

1. ....
2. ....
3. ....

As I reflect on yesterday, what went well and what goals did I accomplish?

_____
_____
_____

Today's self-care goals:

1. ....
2. ....
3. ....

Affirmations I am declaring today!

_____
_____
_____
_____

DATE:

Today I am grateful for:

1. ....
2. ....
3. ....

As I reflect on yesterday, what went well and what goals did I accomplish?

_____

_____

_____

_____

Today's self-care goals:

1. ....
2. ....
3. ....

Affirmations I am declaring today!

_____

_____

_____

_____

_____

SHARE YOUR JOY

Today I am grateful for:

1. ....
2. ....
3. ....

As I reflect on yesterday, what went well and
what goals did I accomplish?

_____

_____

_____

_____

Today's self-care goals:

1. ....
2. ....
3. ....

Affirmations I am declaring today!

_____

_____

_____

_____

DATE:

Today I am grateful for:

1.
2.
3.

As I reflect on yesterday, what went well and what goals did I accomplish?

Today's self-care goals:

1.
2.
3.

Affirmations I am declaring today!

SHARE YOUR JOY

Today I am grateful for:

1. ....

2. ....

3. ....

As I reflect on yesterday, what went well and what goals did I accomplish?

_____

_____

_____

_____

Today's self-care goals:

1. ....

2. ....

3. ....

Affirmations I am declaring today!

_____

_____

_____

_____

_____

DATE:

Today I am grateful for:

1. ....
2. ....
3. ....

As I reflect on yesterday, what went well and what goals did I accomplish?

_____

_____

_____

_____

Today's self-care goals:

1. ....
2. ....
3. ....

Affirmations I am declaring today!

_____

_____

_____

_____

SHARE YOUR JOY

DATE:

Today I am grateful for:

1. _____
2. _____
3. _____

As I reflect on yesterday, what went well and what goals did I accomplish?

_____
_____
_____

Today's self-care goals:

1. _____
2. _____
3. _____

Affirmations I am declaring today!

_____
_____
_____
_____

SHARE YOUR JOY

DATE:

Today I am grateful for:

1. _____

2. _____

3. _____

As I reflect on yesterday, what went well and what goals did I accomplish?

_____

_____

_____

Today's self-care goals:

1. _____

2. _____

3. _____

Affirmations I am declaring today!

_____

_____

_____

_____

SHARE YOUR JOY

Today I am grateful for:

1. _____
2. _____
3. _____

As I reflect on yesterday, what went well and what goals did I accomplish?

_____

_____

_____

Today's self-care goals:

1. _____
2. _____
3. _____

Affirmations I am declaring today!

_____

_____

_____

_____

_____

SHARE YOUR JOY

DATE:

Today I am grateful for:

1.
2.
3.

As I reflect on yesterday, what went well and what goals did I accomplish?

Today's self-care goals:

1.
2.
3.

Affirmations I am declaring today!

SHARE YOUR JOY

Today I am grateful for:

1. ....
2. ....
3. ....

As I reflect on yesterday, what went well and what goals did I accomplish?

_____

_____

_____

_____

Today's self-care goals:

1. ....
2. ....
3. ....

Affirmations I am declaring today!

_____

_____

_____

_____

SHARE YOUR JOY

DATE:

Today I am grateful for:

1. ....
2. ....
3. ....

As I reflect on yesterday, what went well and what goals did I accomplish?

_____

_____

_____

_____

Today's self-care goals:

1. ....
2. ....
3. ....

Affirmations I am declaring today!

_____

_____

_____

_____

_____

SHARE YOUR JOY

Today I am grateful for:

1. ....
2. ....
3. ....

As I reflect on yesterday, what went well and what goals did I accomplish?

_____

_____

_____

_____

Today's self-care goals:

1. ....
2. ....
3. ....

Affirmations I am declaring today!

_____

_____

_____

_____

_____

SHARE YOUR JOY

DATE:

Today I am grateful for:

1. ....
2. ....
3. ....

As I reflect on yesterday, what went well and what goals did I accomplish?

_____

_____

_____

_____

Today's self-care goals:

1. ....
2. ....
3. ....

Affirmations I am declaring today!

_____

_____

_____

_____

_____

SHARE YOUR JOY

Today I am grateful for:

1. ....
2. ....
3. ....

As I reflect on yesterday, what went well and
what goals did I accomplish?

_____

_____

_____

_____

Today's self-care goals:

1. ....
2. ....
3. ....

Affirmations I am declaring today!

_____

_____

_____

_____

_____

SHARE YOUR JOY

Today I am grateful for:

1. ....

2. ....

3. ....

As I reflect on yesterday, what went well and
what goals did I accomplish?

_____

_____

_____

Today's self-care goals:

1. ....

2. ....

3. ....

Affirmations I am declaring today!

_____

_____

_____

_____

SHARE YOUR JOY

DATE:

Today I am grateful for:

1. ....

2. ....

3. ....

As I reflect on yesterday, what went well and what goals did I accomplish?

_____

_____

_____

_____

Today's self-care goals:

1. ....

2. ....

3. ....

Affirmations I am declaring today!

_____

_____

_____

_____

_____

SHARE YOUR JOY

DATE:

Today I am grateful for:

1. ....
2. ....
3. ....

As I reflect on yesterday, what went well and what goals did I accomplish?

_____

_____

_____

_____

Today's self-care goals:

1. ....
2. ....
3. ....

Affirmations I am declaring today!

_____

_____

_____

_____

_____

SHARE YOUR JOY

DATE:

Today I am grateful for:

1. ....
2. ....
3. ....

As I reflect on yesterday, what went well and what goals did I accomplish?

_____

_____

_____

Today's self-care goals:

1. ....
2. ....
3. ....

Affirmations I am declaring today!

_____

_____

_____

_____

SHARE YOUR JOY

DATE:

Today I am grateful for:

1. ....
2. ....
3. ....

As I reflect on yesterday, what went well and what goals did I accomplish?

_____

_____

_____

Today's self-care goals:

1. ....
2. ....
3. ....

Affirmations I am declaring today!

_____

_____

_____

_____

SHARE YOUR JOY

Today I am grateful for:

1. ....
2. ....
3. ....

As I reflect on yesterday, what went well and what goals did I accomplish?

_____

_____

_____

Today's self-care goals:

1. ....
2. ....
3. ....

Affirmations I am declaring today!

_____

_____

_____

_____

SHARE YOUR JOY

DATE:

Today I am grateful for:

1. ....
2. ....
3. ....

As I reflect on yesterday, what went well and what goals did I accomplish?

_____

_____

_____

_____

Today's self-care goals:

1. ....
2. ....
3. ....

Affirmations I am declaring today!

_____

_____

_____

_____

_____

SHARE YOUR JOY

DATE:

Today I am grateful for:

1. ....
2. ....
3. ....

As I reflect on yesterday, what went well and what goals did I accomplish?

_____

_____

_____

_____

Today's self-care goals:

1. ....
2. ....
3. ....

Affirmations I am declaring today!

_____

_____

_____

_____

SHARE YOUR JOY

DATE:

Today I am grateful for:

1. ....
2. ....
3. ....

As I reflect on yesterday, what went well and what goals did I accomplish?

_____

_____

_____

Today's self-care goals:

1. ....
2. ....
3. ....

Affirmations I am declaring today!

_____

_____

_____

_____

SHARE YOUR JOY

Today I am grateful for:

1.
2.
3.

As I reflect on yesterday, what went well and what goals did I accomplish?

Today's self-care goals:

1.
2.
3.

Affirmations I am declaring today!

SHARE YOUR JOY

Today I am grateful for:

1.
2.
3.

As I reflect on yesterday, what went well and what goals did I accomplish?

Today's self-care goals:

1.
2.
3.

Affirmations I am declaring today!

SHARE YOUR JOY

Today I am grateful for:

1. ....
2. ....
3. ....

As I reflect on yesterday, what went well and what goals did I accomplish?

_____

_____

_____

Today's self-care goals:

1. ....
2. ....
3. ....

Affirmations I am declaring today!

_____

_____

_____

_____

SHARE YOUR JOY

DATE:

Today I am grateful for:

1. ....
2. ....
3. ....

As I reflect on yesterday, what went well and what goals did I accomplish?

_____

_____

_____

_____

Today's self-care goals:

1. ....
2. ....
3. ....

Affirmations I am declaring today!

_____

_____

_____

_____

SHARE YOUR JOY

Today I am grateful for:

1. ....
2. ....
3. ....

As I reflect on yesterday, what went well and what goals did I accomplish?

_____

_____

_____

_____

Today's self-care goals:

1. ....
2. ....
3. ....

Affirmations I am declaring today!

_____

_____

_____

_____

_____

SHARE YOUR JOY

DATE:

Today I am grateful for:

1. _____
2. _____
3. _____

As I reflect on yesterday, what went well and what goals did I accomplish?

_____
_____
_____

Today's self-care goals:

1. _____
2. _____
3. _____

Affirmations I am declaring today!

_____
_____
_____
_____

SHARE YOUR JOY

DATE:

Today I am grateful for:

1. ....
2. ....
3. ....

As I reflect on yesterday, what went well and what goals did I accomplish?

_____

_____

_____

Today's self-care goals:

1. ....
2. ....
3. ....

Affirmations I am declaring today!

_____

_____

_____

_____

SHARE YOUR JOY

DATE:

Today I am grateful for:

1. ....
2. ....
3. ....

As I reflect on yesterday, what went well and
what goals did I accomplish?

_____

_____

_____

_____

Today's self-care goals:

1. ....
2. ....
3. ....

Affirmations I am declaring today!

_____

_____

_____

_____

_____

SHARE YOUR JOY

Today I am grateful for:

1. ....
2. ....
3. ....

As I reflect on yesterday, what went well and what goals did I accomplish?

_____

_____

_____

_____

Today's self-care goals:

1. ....
2. ....
3. ....

Affirmations I am declaring today!

_____

_____

_____

_____

_____

SHARE YOUR JOY

DATE:

Today I am grateful for:

1. ....
2. ....
3. ....

As I reflect on yesterday, what went well and what goals did I accomplish?

_____

_____

_____

_____

Today's self-care goals:

1. ....
2. ....
3. ....

Affirmations I am declaring today!

_____

_____

_____

_____

_____

SHARE YOUR JOY

DATE:

Today I am grateful for:

1. ....
2. ....
3. ....

As I reflect on yesterday, what went well and what goals did I accomplish?

_____
_____
_____

Today's self-care goals:

1. ....
2. ....
3. ....

Affirmations I am declaring today!

_____
_____
_____
_____

SHARE YOUR JOY

DATE:

Today I am grateful for:

1. ....
2. ....
3. ....

As I reflect on yesterday, what went well and
what goals did I accomplish?

_____

_____

_____

Today's self-care goals:

1. ....
2. ....
3. ....

Affirmations I am declaring today!

_____

_____

_____

_____

_____

SHARE YOUR JOY

DATE:

Today I am grateful for:

1. ....
2. ....
3. ....

As I reflect on yesterday, what went well and what goals did I accomplish?

_____

_____

_____

_____

Today's self-care goals:

1. ....
2. ....
3. ....

Affirmations I am declaring today!

_____

_____

_____

_____

SHARE YOUR JOY

Today I am grateful for:

1. ....
2. ....
3. ....

As I reflect on yesterday, what went well and what goals did I accomplish?

_____

_____

_____

Today's self-care goals:

1. ....
2. ....
3. ....

Affirmations I am declaring today!

_____

_____

_____

_____

SHARE YOUR JOY

Today I am grateful for:

1. ....

2. ....

3. ....

As I reflect on yesterday, what went well and what goals did I accomplish?

_____

_____

_____

Today's self-care goals:

1. ....

2. ....

3. ....

Affirmations I am declaring today!

_____

_____

_____

_____

_____

SHARE YOUR JOY

Today I am grateful for:

1. ....
2. ....
3. ....

As I reflect on yesterday, what went well and what goals did I accomplish?

_____

_____

_____

Today's self-care goals:

1. ....
2. ....
3. ....

Affirmations I am declaring today!

_____

_____

_____

_____

SHARE YOUR JOY

DATE:

Today I am grateful for:

1.
2.
3.

As I reflect on yesterday, what went well and what goals did I accomplish?

_____

_____

_____

_____

Today's self-care goals:

1.
2.
3.

Affirmations I am declaring today!

_____

_____

_____

_____

SHARE YOUR JOY

DATE:

Today I am grateful for:

1. ....
2. ....
3. ....

As I reflect on yesterday, what went well and what goals did I accomplish?

_____

_____

_____

Today's self-care goals:

1. ....
2. ....
3. ....

Affirmations I am declaring today!

_____

_____

_____

_____

SHARE YOUR JOY

Today I am grateful for:

1. ....
2. ....
3. ....

As I reflect on yesterday, what went well and what goals did I accomplish?

_____

_____

_____

_____

Today's self-care goals:

1. ....
2. ....
3. ....

Affirmations I am declaring today!

_____

_____

_____

_____

SHARE YOUR JOY

Today I am grateful for:

1. ....

2. ....

3. ....

As I reflect on yesterday, what went well and what goals did I accomplish?

_____

_____

_____

_____

Today's self-care goals:

1. ....

2. ....

3. ....

Affirmations I am declaring today!

_____

_____

_____

_____

SHARE YOUR JOY

DATE:

Today I am grateful for:

1. _____
2. _____
3. _____

As I reflect on yesterday, what went well and what goals did I accomplish?

_____
_____
_____
_____

Today's self-care goals:

1. _____
2. _____
3. _____

Affirmations I am declaring today!

_____
_____
_____
_____

SHARE YOUR JOY

DATE:

Today I am grateful for:

1. _____
2. _____
3. _____

As I reflect on yesterday, what went well and what goals did I accomplish?

_____
_____
_____

Today's self-care goals:

1. _____
2. _____
3. _____

Affirmations I am declaring today!

_____
_____
_____
_____

SHARE YOUR JOY

Today I am grateful for:

1. ....

2. ....

3. ....

As I reflect on yesterday, what went well and what goals did I accomplish?

_____

_____

_____

_____

Today's self-care goals:

1. ....

2. ....

3. ....

Affirmations I am declaring today!

_____

_____

_____

_____

_____

SHARE YOUR JOY

DATE:

Today I am grateful for:

1. ....
2. ....
3. ....

As I reflect on yesterday, what went well and what goals did I accomplish?

_____

_____

_____

Today's self-care goals:

1. ....
2. ....
3. ....

Affirmations I am declaring today!

_____

_____

_____

_____

SHARE YOUR JOY

DATE:

Today I am grateful for:

1. ....
2. ....
3. ....

As I reflect on yesterday, what went well and what goals did I accomplish?

_____

_____

_____

_____

Today's self-care goals:

1. ....
2. ....
3. ....

Affirmations I am declaring today!

_____

_____

_____

_____

_____

SHARE YOUR JOY

DATE:

Today I am grateful for:

1. ....
2. ....
3. ....

As I reflect on yesterday, what went well and what goals did I accomplish?

_____

_____

_____

Today's self-care goals:

1. ....
2. ....
3. ....

Affirmations I am declaring today!

_____

_____

_____

_____

SHARE YOUR JOY

Today I am grateful for:

1. ....
2. ....
3. ....

As I reflect on yesterday, what went well and what goals did I accomplish?

_____

_____

_____

Today's self-care goals:

1. ....
2. ....
3. ....

Affirmations I am declaring today!

_____

_____

_____

_____

SHARE YOUR JOY

DATE:

Today I am grateful for:

1. ....
2. ....
3. ....

As I reflect on yesterday, what went well and what goals did I accomplish?

_____

_____

_____

_____

Today's self-care goals:

1. ....
2. ....
3. ....

Affirmations I am declaring today!

_____

_____

_____

_____

SHARE YOUR JOY

DATE:

Today I am grateful for:

1. ....
2. ....
3. ....

As I reflect on yesterday, what went well and what goals did I accomplish?

_____

_____

_____

_____

Today's self-care goals:

1. ....
2. ....
3. ....

Affirmations I am declaring today!

_____

_____

_____

_____

SHARE YOUR JOY

DATE:

Today I am grateful for:

1. ....
2. ....
3. ....

As I reflect on yesterday, what went well and what goals did I accomplish?

_____

_____

_____

Today's self-care goals:

1. ....
2. ....
3. ....

Affirmations I am declaring today!

_____

_____

_____

_____

SHARE YOUR JOY

Today I am grateful for:

1.
2.
3.

As I reflect on yesterday, what went well and what goals did I accomplish?

Today's self-care goals:

1.
2.
3.

Affirmations I am declaring today!

SHARE YOUR JOY

DATE:

Today I am grateful for:

1. _____
2. _____
3. _____

As I reflect on yesterday, what went well and what goals did I accomplish?

_____

_____

_____

Today's self-care goals:

1. _____
2. _____
3. _____

Affirmations I am declaring today!

_____

_____

_____

_____

SHARE YOUR JOY

DATE:

Today I am grateful for:

1. ....
2. ....
3. ....

As I reflect on yesterday, what went well and what goals did I accomplish?

_____

_____

_____

Today's self-care goals:

1. ....
2. ....
3. ....

Affirmations I am declaring today!

_____

_____

_____

_____

SHARE YOUR JOY

Today I am grateful for:

1.
2.
3.

As I reflect on yesterday, what went well and what goals did I accomplish?

Today's self-care goals:

1.
2.
3.

Affirmations I am declaring today!

SHARE YOUR JOY

DATE:

Today I am grateful for:

1. ....
2. ....
3. ....

As I reflect on yesterday, what went well and what goals did I accomplish?

_____

_____

_____

Today's self-care goals:

1. ....
2. ....
3. ....

Affirmations I am declaring today!

_____

_____

_____

_____

SHARE YOUR JOY

DATE:

Today I am grateful for:

1. _____
2. _____
3. _____

As I reflect on yesterday, what went well and what goals did I accomplish?

_____
_____
_____
_____

Today's self-care goals:

1. _____
2. _____
3. _____

Affirmations I am declaring today!

_____
_____
_____
_____
_____

SHARE YOUR JOY

DATE:

Today I am grateful for:

1. ....
2. ....
3. ....

As I reflect on yesterday, what went well and what goals did I accomplish?

_____

_____

_____

_____

Today's self-care goals:

1. ....
2. ....
3. ....

Affirmations I am declaring today!

_____

_____

_____

_____

SHARE YOUR JOY

DATE:

Today I am grateful for:

1. ....
2. ....
3. ....

As I reflect on yesterday, what went well and what goals did I accomplish?

_____

_____

_____

Today's self-care goals:

1. ....
2. ....
3. ....

Affirmations I am declaring today!

_____

_____

_____

_____

SHARE YOUR JOY

Today I am grateful for:

1. ....

2. ....

3. ....

As I reflect on yesterday, what went well and what goals did I accomplish?

_____

_____

_____

Today's self-care goals:

1. ....

2. ....

3. ....

Affirmations I am declaring today!

_____

_____

_____

_____

DATE:

Today I am grateful for:

1. ....
2. ....
3. ....

As I reflect on yesterday, what went well and what goals did I accomplish?

_____

_____

_____

Today's self-care goals:

1. ....
2. ....
3. ....

Affirmations I am declaring today!

_____

_____

_____

_____

SHARE YOUR JOY

Today I am grateful for:

1. ....
2. ....
3. ....

As I reflect on yesterday, what went well and what goals did I accomplish?

_____

_____

_____

_____

Today's self-care goals:

1. ....
2. ....
3. ....

Affirmations I am declaring today!

_____

_____

_____

_____

SHARE YOUR JOY

DATE:

Today I am grateful for:

1. ....
2. ....
3. ....

As I reflect on yesterday, what went well and what goals did I accomplish?

_____

_____

_____

_____

Today's self-care goals:

1. ....
2. ....
3. ....

Affirmations I am declaring today!

_____

_____

_____

_____

SHARE YOUR JOY

DATE:

Today I am grateful for:

1. ....
2. ....
3. ....

As I reflect on yesterday, what went well and what goals did I accomplish?

_____

_____

_____

_____

Today's self-care goals:

1. --
2. --
3. --

Affirmations I am declaring today!

_____

_____

_____

_____

_____

SHARE YOUR JOY

DATE:

Today I am grateful for:

1. _____
2. _____
3. _____

As I reflect on yesterday, what went well and what goals did I accomplish?

_____

_____

_____

_____

Today's self-care goals:

1. _____
2. _____
3. _____

Affirmations I am declaring today!

_____

_____

_____

_____

SHARE YOUR JOY

Today I am grateful for:

1. ....

2. ....

3. ....

As I reflect on yesterday, what went well and what goals did I accomplish?

_____

_____

_____

Today's self-care goals:

1. ....

2. ....

3. ....

Affirmations I am declaring today!

_____

_____

_____

_____

SHARE YOUR JOY

DATE:

Today I am grateful for:

1.
2.
3.

As I reflect on yesterday, what went well and what goals did I accomplish?

Today's self-care goals:

1.
2.
3.

Affirmations I am declaring today!

SHARE YOUR JOY

DATE:

Today I am grateful for:

1. ....
2. ....
3. ....

As I reflect on yesterday, what went well and what goals did I accomplish?

_____
_____
_____
_____

Today's self-care goals:

1. ....
2. ....
3. ....

Affirmations I am declaring today!

_____
_____
_____
_____

SHARE YOUR JOY

DATE:

Today I am grateful for:

1. ....
2. ....
3. ....

As I reflect on yesterday, what went well and what goals did I accomplish?

_____

_____

_____

Today's self-care goals:

1. ....
2. ....
3. ....

Affirmations I am declaring today!

_____

_____

_____

_____

SHARE YOUR JOY

DATE:

Today I am grateful for:

1. ....
2. ....
3. ....

As I reflect on yesterday, what went well and what goals did I accomplish?

_____

_____

_____

Today's self-care goals:

1. ....
2. ....
3. ....

Affirmations I am declaring today!

_____

_____

_____

_____

SHARE YOUR JOY

DATE:

Today I am grateful for:

1. ....
2. ....
3. ....

As I reflect on yesterday, what went well and what goals did I accomplish?

_____

_____

_____

_____

Today's self-care goals:

1. ....
2. ....
3. ....

Affirmations I am declaring today!

_____

_____

_____

_____

_____

SHARE YOUR JOY

Today I am grateful for:

1. _____
2. _____
3. _____

As I reflect on yesterday, what went well and what goals did I accomplish?

_____
_____
_____

Today's self-care goals:

1. _____
2. _____
3. _____

Affirmations I am declaring today!

_____
_____
_____
_____
_____

SHARE YOUR JOY

Today I am grateful for:

1. ....
2. ....
3. ....

As I reflect on yesterday, what went well and what goals did I accomplish?

_____

_____

_____

_____

Today's self-care goals:

1. ....
2. ....
3. ....

Affirmations I am declaring today!

_____

_____

_____

_____

SHARE YOUR JOY

Today I am grateful for:

1. ....
2. ....
3. ....

As I reflect on yesterday, what went well and what goals did I accomplish?

_____

_____

_____

_____

Today's self-care goals:

1. ....
2. ....
3. ....

Affirmations I am declaring today!

_____

_____

_____

_____

_____

SHARE YOUR JOY

DATE:

Today I am grateful for:

1. ....
2. ....
3. ....

As I reflect on yesterday, what went well and what goals did I accomplish?

_____
_____
_____

Today's self-care goals:

1. ....
2. ....
3. ....

Affirmations I am declaring today!

_____
_____
_____
_____

SHARE YOUR JOY

DATE:

Today I am grateful for:

1. ....
2. ....
3. ....

As I reflect on yesterday, what went well and what goals did I accomplish?

_____
_____
_____
_____

Today's self-care goals:

1. ....
2. ....
3. ....

Affirmations I am declaring today!

_____
_____
_____
_____
_____

SHARE YOUR JOY

DATE:

Today I am grateful for:

1.
2.
3.

As I reflect on yesterday, what went well and what goals did I accomplish?

Today's self-care goals:

1.
2.
3.

Affirmations I am declaring today!

SHARE YOUR JOY

DATE:

Today I am grateful for:

1. ....
2. ....
3. ....

As I reflect on yesterday, what went well and what goals did I accomplish?

_____

_____

_____

Today's self-care goals:

1. ....
2. ....
3. ....

Affirmations I am declaring today!

_____

_____

_____

_____

SHARE YOUR JOY

DATE:

Today I am grateful for:

1. ....
2. ....
3. ....

As I reflect on yesterday, what went well and what goals did I accomplish?

_____

_____

_____

_____

Today's self-care goals:

1. ....
2. ....
3. ....

Affirmations I am declaring today!

_____

_____

_____

_____

SHARE YOUR JOY

DATE:

Today I am grateful for:

1. ....
2. ....
3. ....

As I reflect on yesterday, what went well and what goals did I accomplish?

_____

_____

_____

_____

Today's self-care goals:

1. ....
2. ....
3. ....

Affirmations I am declaring today!

_____

_____

_____

_____

_____

SHARE YOUR JOY

Today I am grateful for:

1. ....
2. ....
3. ....

As I reflect on yesterday, what went well and what goals did I accomplish?

_____

_____

_____

_____

Today's self-care goals:

1. ....
2. ....
3. ....

Affirmations I am declaring today!

_____

_____

_____

_____

SHARE YOUR JOY

DATE:

Today I am grateful for:

1. ....
2. ....
3. ....

As I reflect on yesterday, what went well and what goals did I accomplish?

_____

_____

_____

Today's self-care goals:

1. ....
2. ....
3. ....

Affirmations I am declaring today!

_____

_____

_____

_____

SHARE YOUR JOY

DATE:

Today I am grateful for:

1. ....

2. ....

3. ....

As I reflect on yesterday, what went well and what goals did I accomplish?

_____

_____

_____

_____

Today's self-care goals:

1. ....

2. ....

3. ....

Affirmations I am declaring today!

_____

_____

_____

_____

_____

SHARE YOUR JOY

DATE:

Today I am grateful for:

1. ....
2. ....
3. ....

As I reflect on yesterday, what went well and what goals did I accomplish?

_____

_____

_____

Today's self-care goals:

1. ....
2. ....
3. ....

Affirmations I am declaring today!

_____

_____

_____

_____

SHARE YOUR JOY

DATE:

Today I am grateful for:

1. _____
2. _____
3. _____

As I reflect on yesterday, what went well and
what goals did I accomplish?

_____
_____
_____
_____

Today's self-care goals:

1. _____
2. _____
3. _____

Affirmations I am declaring today!

_____
_____
_____
_____
_____

SHARE YOUR JOY

DATE:

Today I am grateful for:

1. _____
2. _____
3. _____

As I reflect on yesterday, what went well and what goals did I accomplish?

_____
_____
_____
_____

Today's self-care goals:

1. _____
2. _____
3. _____

Affirmations I am declaring today!

_____
_____
_____
_____

SHARE YOUR JOY